7 Beautiful and Easy Doily Crochet Patterns

Simple Crochet Doily for Beginners

Table of Content

Introduction

Many people who crochet in modern times avoided crocheting doilies for a long time. They wonder where they will use them. They assume that all crochet doilies are made with thread and that thread crochet is difficult—both of which are false assumptions. They get so excited about making contemporary things that they don't get interested in making doilies. But at some point in your crochet journey, you might want to explore the joy of doily making.

Doilies are circular, making them great projects for meditative crochet. Doilies, like crochet mandalas, can be used as decoration on tables or even framed as beautiful wall art. Alternatively, doilies can serve as the centerpiece for wearable designs including hair

accessories, they can be worked up in alternative materials like t-shirt yarn for use as rugs, or they can be wrapped around stones and other up-cycled materials. Many people have been inspired to make doily dresses for proms and other special events. Doilies can be tons of fun.

Here are seven crochet doily patterns, some of them vintage and some of them fresh, to inspire you to get started with doily making and design.

Pointed Harmony Doily Crochet Pattern

This crochet doily pattern is what many of us think of as a traditional doily pattern. It is a relatively advanced doily pattern, using special long stitches along with cluster stitches to create a great textured openwork design.

People who are comfortable working in thread crochet to create doilies and want to take on a challenge will find this to be a fun design.

How to make

Size: About 13 inches
Materials: Size 20 Mercerized Crochet Cotton: White (400 yds)
Crochet Hook: No. 12 (1.00 mm).
Abbreviations

ch	chain	rnd	round
dc	double crochet	sc	single crochet(s)
hdc	half double crochet	sl st(s)	slip stitch(es)
lp(s)	loop(s)	sp(s)	space(s)
rem	remaining	st(s)	stitch(es)
rep	repeat	yo	yarn over

Special Stitches
Double Treble Cluster (dtr-cl): Keeping last loop of each st on hook, dtr in sts or sps indicated, yo and pull through all loops on hook.
Long Treble (L-tr): Yo hook 5 times, insert hook in st or sp indicated, and work off in twos as for tr-tr.

Triple Treble (tr-tr): Yo hook 4 times, insert hook in st or sp indicated, yo, draw lp through, [yo, draw through 2 lps on hook] 5 times.

DOILY

Work tightly for best results.

Rnd 1: Starting at center, ch 9, join with sl st to first ch to form ring; ch 1, 16 sc in ring; join with sl st to first sc.

Rnd 2: Ch 4 (counts as first dc and ch 1), dc in next sc, (ch 1, dc in next sc) 14 times, ch 1, join with sl st to first dc.

Rnd 3: Ch 3 (counts as first dc now and throughout), (2 dc in next sp, dc in next dc, ch 5, sl st in last dc (picot), 2 dc in next sp, dc in next dc) around; join.

Rnd 4: Ch 16, (tr in center dc between next 2 picots, ch 11) around; join to 5th st of ch-16.

Rnd 5: Ch 1, sc in same st, (13 sc in next sp, sc in next tr) around; join with sl st to first sc.

Rnd 6: Ch 7, 2-dtr-cl in same st, * (ch 6, sl st in 5th st from hook *(picot)*) 3 times, ch 3, skip 6 sc, sc in next sc, ch 7, picot, (ch 6, picot) twice, ch 2, skip 6 sc, 3-dtr-cl in next sc; rep from * around; join to first cluster.

Rnd 7: Ch 27, (tr in next cluster, ch 22) around; join to 5th st of ch-27.

Rnd 8: Sc in next sp, ** (ch 2, sc) 13 times across same sp, ch 1, turn, sc in first ch-2 lp, (ch 2, sc in next lp) 12 times, * ch 1, turn, sc in first lp, (ch 2, sc in next lp) across *(1 less lp than last row)*; rep from * 9 times; ch 1, turn, sc in first lp, ch 1, hdc in next lp. Finish off leaving 2" long end.

Rnd 9: Sc in bar of hdc, * (2 sc in next sp downside of point) 11 times, sc in next sp, sc in next tr, sc in first sp on next point, (2 sc in next sp) 6 times, ch 8, turn, L- tr in sc between points, ch 8, sl st in 13th sc up next point, ch 1, turn, (5 sc, ch-5 picot. 5 sc) in first sp, sc in L-tr, (5 sc, picot, 5 sc) in next sp, (2 sc in next sp on point) 5 times, sc in next *(tip)* sp, ch 19, turn, dc in center sc between picots, ch 19, sl st in 11th sc up next point, ch 1, turn, (11 sc, picot, 11 sc) in first sp, sc in dc, (11 sc, picot, 11 sc) in next sp, 2 sc in same tip sp on point; rep from * around; end with sc in tip sp.

Rnd 10: Ch 23, * (tr-tr, ch 9, tr-tr) in center sc between picots, ch 20, dc in sc at tip of next point, ch 20; rep from * around; join to 3rd st of ch-23.

Rnd 11: Ch 1, sc in same st, (23 sc in next sp, sc in tr-tr, 11 sc in next sp, sc in next tr-tr, 23 sc in next sp, sc in next dc) around; join to first sc.

Rnd 12: Sl st in next sc, * sc in next sc, (ch 2, skip next sc, sc in next sc) 10 times, ch 5, sl st in 5th ch from hook *(picot)*, ch 1, skip 3 sc, dc in next sc, (ch 5, picot, ch 1, skip next sc, dc in next sc) 4 times, ch 5, picot, ch 1, skip 3 sc, sc in next sc, (ch 2, skip next sc, sc in next sc) 10 times, skip 3 sc in angle; rep from * around; join to first sc.

Rnd 13: * Sc in next ch-2 lp, (ch 2, sc in next lp) 8 times, (ch 6, picot, ch 2, tr in next dc) 5 times, ch 6, picot, ch 2, skip ch-2 lp, sc in next Ip, (ch 2, sc in next lp) 8 times; rep from * around; join to first sc.

Rnd 14: * Sc in next ch-2 Ip, (ch 2, sc in next lp) 6 times, (ch 7, picot, ch 3, tr in next tr) 3 times, ch 7, picot, ch 3, tr in same tr, (ch 7, picot, ch 3, tr in next tr) twice, ch 7, picot, ch 3, skip ch-2 lp, sc in next lp, (ch 2, sc in next lp) 6 times; rep from * around; join to first sc.

Rnd 15: * Sc in next ch-2 lp, (ch 2, sc in next lp) 4 times, (ch 8, picot, ch 4, tr in next tr) 3 times, ch 8, picot, ch 9, picot, ch 4, tr in next tr, (ch 8, picot, ch 4, tr in next tr) twice, ch 8, picot, ch 4, skip ch-2 lp, sc in next Ip, (ch 2, sc in next lp) 4 times; rep from * around; join to first sc.

Rnd 16: * Sc in next ch-2 lp, (ch 2, sc in next lp) twice, (ch 9, picot, ch 5, tr in next tr) 3 times, ch 9, picot, ch 5, tr in center st between next 2 picots, ch 9, picot, ch 5, tr in same st, (ch 9, picot, ch 5, tr in next tr) 3 times, ch 9, picot, ch 5, skip ch-2 lp, sc in next lp, (ch 2, sc in next lp) twice; rep from * around; join to first sc. Finish off and weave in ends.

Rnd 17: With **right side** facing, join to final tr on any pattern, ch 5, * tr in first tr on next pattern, (ch 12, tr in next tr) 3 times, ch 7, (tr, ch 7, tr) in next picot, ch 7, tr in next tr, (ch 12, tr in next tr) 4 times; rep from * around; join to first ch-5.

Rnd 18: (7 sc, ch-5 picot, 7 sc) in each ch-12 sp around; (4 sc, picot, 4 sc) in each ch-7 sp; join with sl st to first sc. Finish off and weave in ends.

Stretch and pin doily right-side-down in a true circle. Steam and press dry through a cloth.

Spiral Doily Vintage Crochet Pattern

Although most doilies that you will come across are worked entirely in the round as pure circles, you will occasionally discover an amazing doily like this one that is comprised of motifs. This is a vintage thread crochet pattern comprised of spiral medallion motifs that are stitched together to create the full doily.

How to make
Materials:

- 1 Ball, DMC Cebelia Size 10 Crochet Thread
- 1.25 mm Crochet Hook
- Small Darning Needle

Notes:

The pattern for the medallions is an interpretation of a pattern found in Piecework Magazine Presents, A Facsimile Edition Of, Weldon's Practical Needlework, Volume 6, called "Passementerie Dress Trimming", original author unknown. Copyright 2002, Interweave Press, Inc., Loveland, Colorado.

Each medallion can be crocheted individually and then sewn together, or can be crocheted to the surrounding medallions as it is being made. It is suggested that medallions are joined as they are made.

Key:

Symbol	Term	Abbreviation
⬯	Chain	ch
⊞	Single Crochet	sc
⊞	Single Crochet Back Loop Only	sc blo
⊡	Slip Stitch	sl st
⊤	Treble Crochet	tr

Instructions for medallions:
(Make 7)
Part 1 – ch 7; join in a round with a sl st through the first chain to form a ring

Part 2 – 12 sc in the ring that was just made; sl st into the first sc

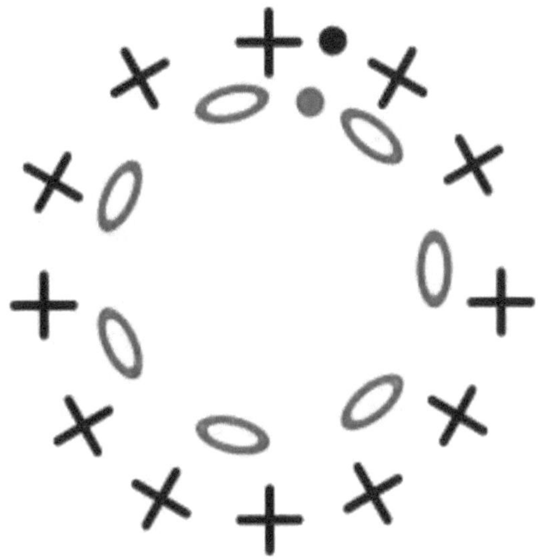

Part 3 (First Arm)
    a. ch 14; turn work
    b. sc into the back bump of the last ch made
    c. sc 21 around the 13 chain just made
    d. sc into the next sc from Part 2; turn work
    e. sc into the back loop of the of the 21 sc just made in Row 3, part c
    f. ch 1; turn work

g. [sc into the back loop of the next 4 sc from Part 3.d; ch 4] 4 times; sc into the back loop of the last sc on the arm

h. sc into the next sc from Part 2

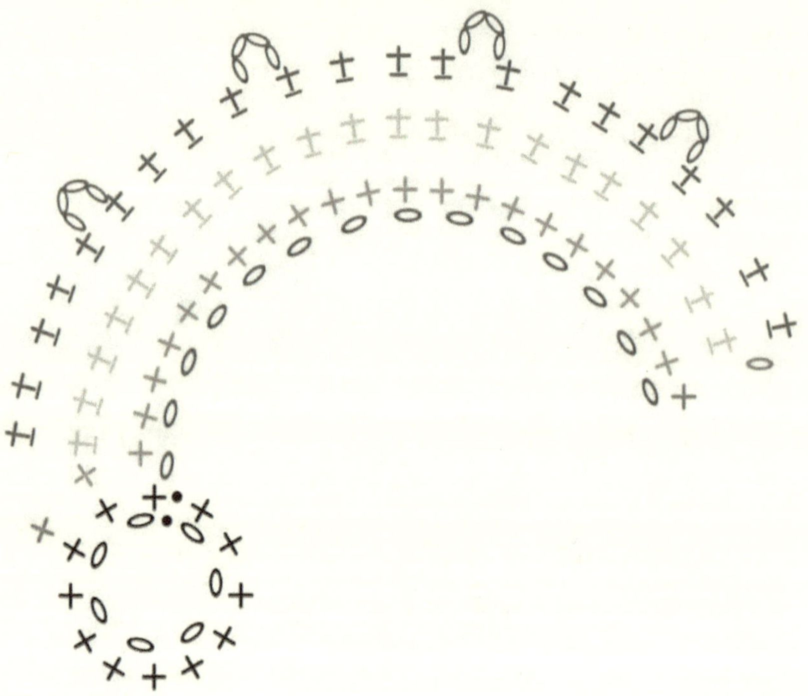

Part 4 (Second through Fifth Arms)
   a. ch 14
   b. sl st into the third picot made on the previous leg
   c. sc 21 over the last ch 14
   d. sc into the next sc from Part 2; turn work
   e. sc into the back loop of the 21 sc made in Part 4.c
   f. ch 1; turn work

g. [sc into the back loop of the next 4 sc from Part
   4.e; ch 4] 4 times; sc into the back loop of the
   last sc on the arm
h. sc into the next sc from Part 2
(Complete this section a total of 4 times.)

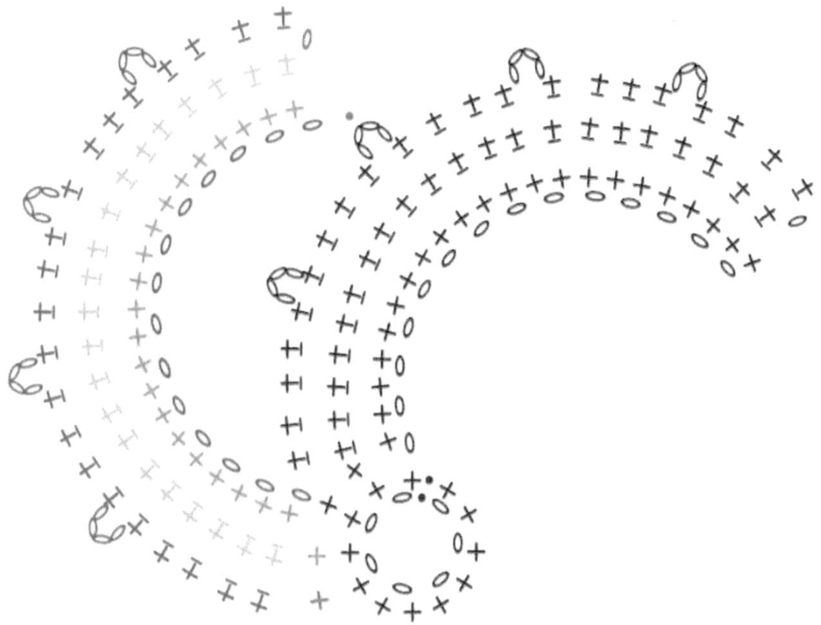

Part 5 (Sixth Arm)
   a. ch 14
   b. sl st into the third picot made on the previous
      leg
   c. sc 21 over the last ch 14
   d. sc into the next sc from Part 2; turn work
   e. sc into the back loop of the 21 sc made in Part
      5.c
   f. ch 1; turn work

g. [sc into the back loop of the next 4 sc from Part 5.e; ch 4] 2 times; ch 2; sl st through the end of the first arm made (This can be tricky, try aiming for the stitch from Part 3.b); ch 1; sc into the back loop of the next 4 sc from Part 5.e; ch 4; sc into the back loop of the last 5 sc on the arm

h. sl st into the last sc from Part 2

Pull thread through and cut leaving ~6" tail.

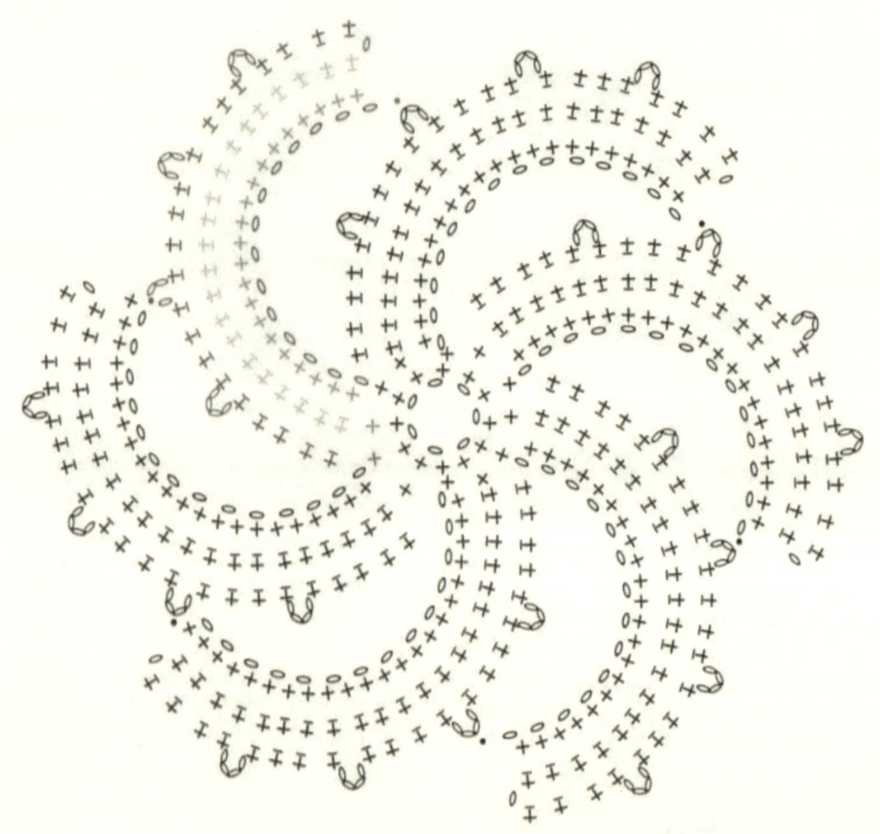

Instructions for joining medallions:

Medallions can be joined after each one is made, or as each successive medallion is made. Personally I prefer to join each new medallion as I make it.

<u>For joining to a single medallion</u>

  i.   Complete through Part 3.f of the second medallion

  ii.   sc into the back loop of the closest 4 sc from previous row starting with the one closest to the hook; ch 4;

        sc into the back loop of the next 4 sc on the arm; ch 2; ch 1 through the first loop of an arm of the first medallion; ch 1; (It doesn't matter which arm as long as the line up correctly.)

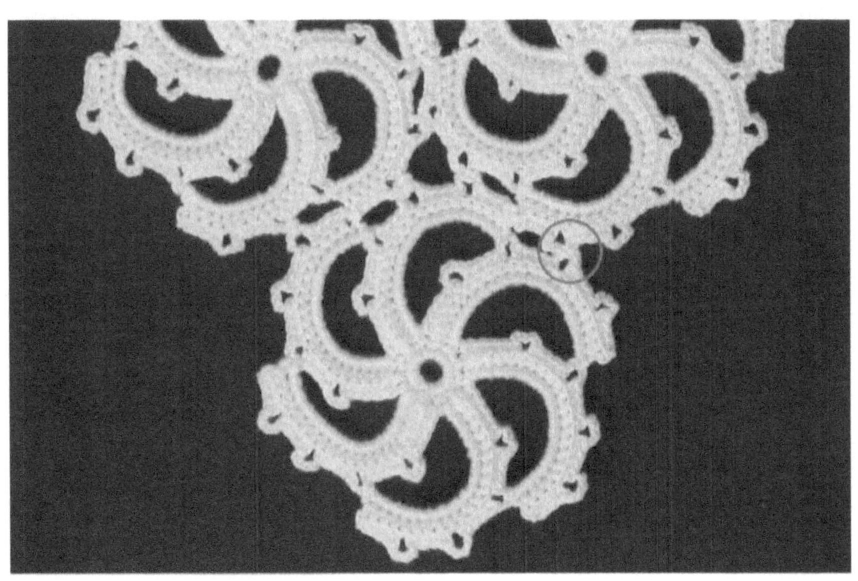

Be sure that the medallions will have the same face forward as you sew them together, because it will be obvious latter on if you have one facing a different direction.

iii. [sc into the back loop of the next 4 sc on the arm; ch 4] twice; sc into the back loop of the last 5 sc on the arm; sc into the next sc from the initial ring (This completes the first arm of the second medallion.)

iv. Continue working through Part4.e of the next arm

v. sc into the outside tip of the arm on the first medallion that you have already attached to (Be careful not to add a twist to the medallions.)

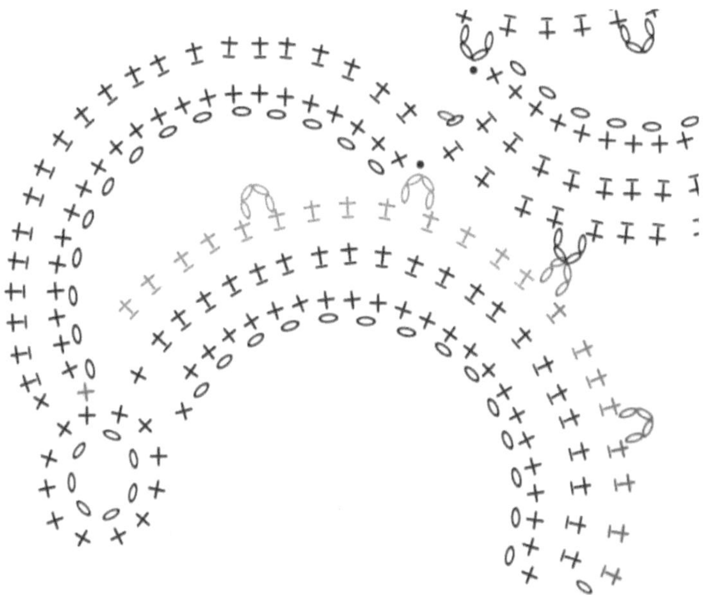

vi.   sc into the back loop of the closest 4 sc from previous row starting with the one closest to the hook;

    -    2; ch 1 through the second ch 4 space on the next leg on the first medallion; ch 1; sc into the back loop of the next 4 sc on the arm you are currently working on

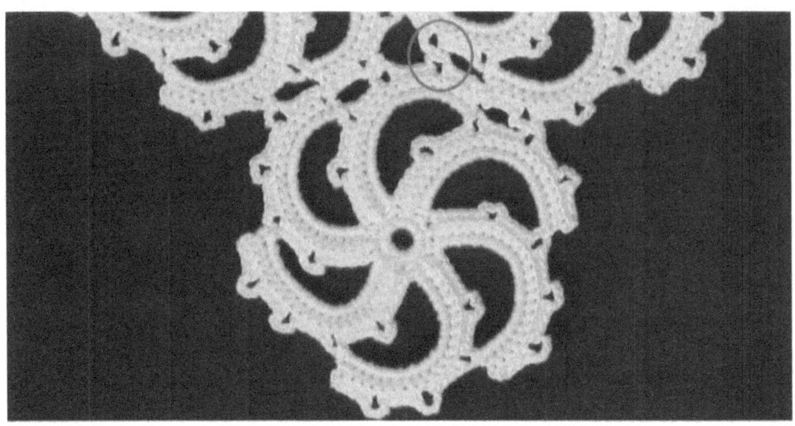

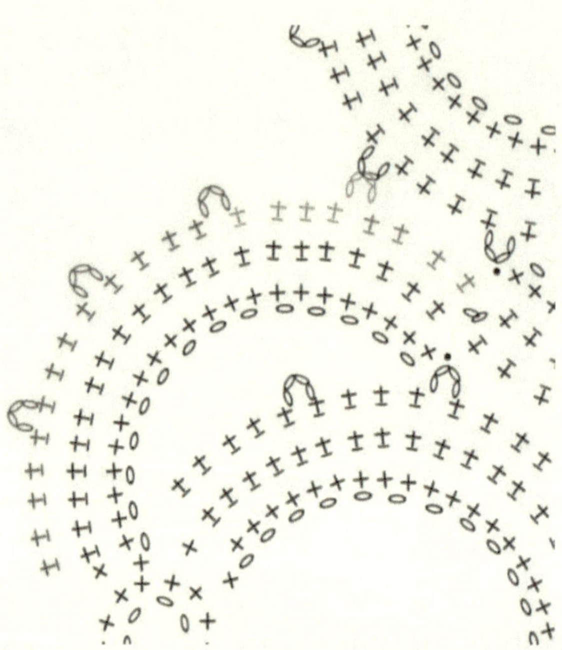

vii.   [Ch 4; sc into the back loop of the next 4 sc] x 3,
         sc into the back loop of the last sc on the arm
viii.   Sc into the next sc from Part 2
 ix.   Complete the rest of the medallion as before

For joining to multiple medallions
- Start as if you are joining to a single medallion,
instead of continuing with Step g,
  • ch 2; ch 1 through the first loop on the arm of
    the next medallion; ch 1; sc into the back loop
    of the next 4 sc on the medallion that you are
    building.
  • [ch 4; sc into the back loop of the next 4 sc] x 2,
    sc into the back loop of the last sc on the arm
  • Continue from Part 4.h of the current arm
    through 4.e of the next arm.

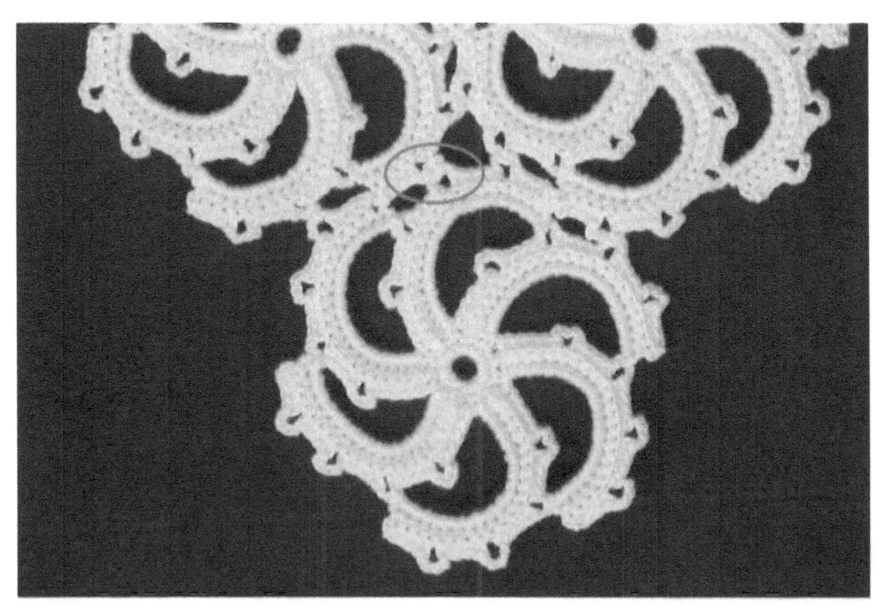

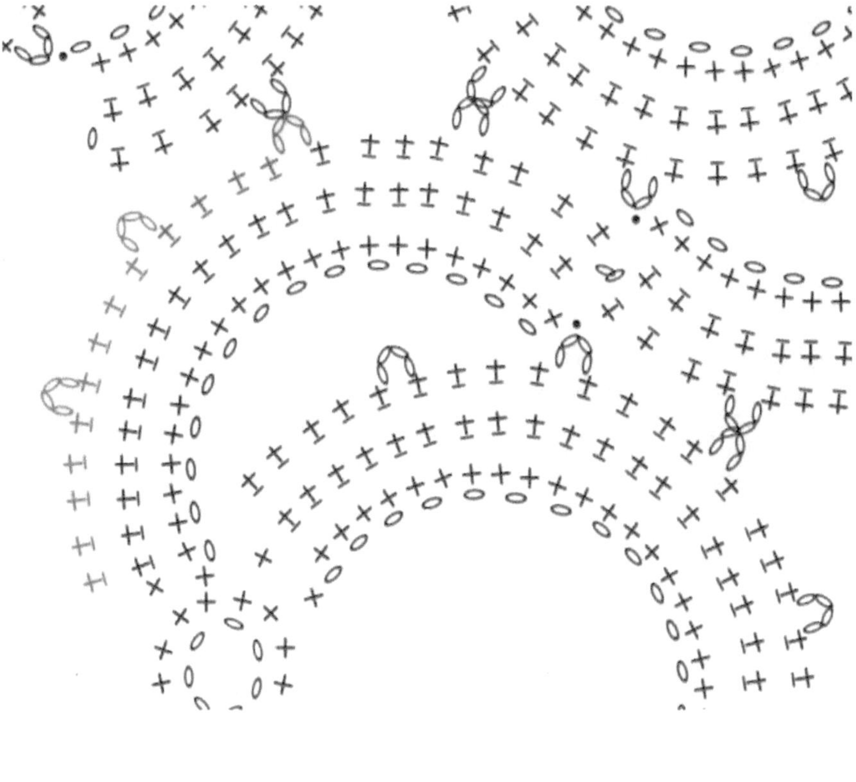

- Continue on as you did joining to the first medallion from Step v
- Continue like this until you have joined to as many medallions as you wish.
- After you have finished attaching to as many medallions as you wish, complete the rest of the medallion starting with Part 4.g after the first picot.

After all medallions are finished weave in and trim ends.

Instructions for edging:

After all the medallions have been made and attached together, and after all of the ends have been woven in:

Round 1 – With the right side of the doily facing you, choose a space between two medallions and attach thread to the picot on the left side.

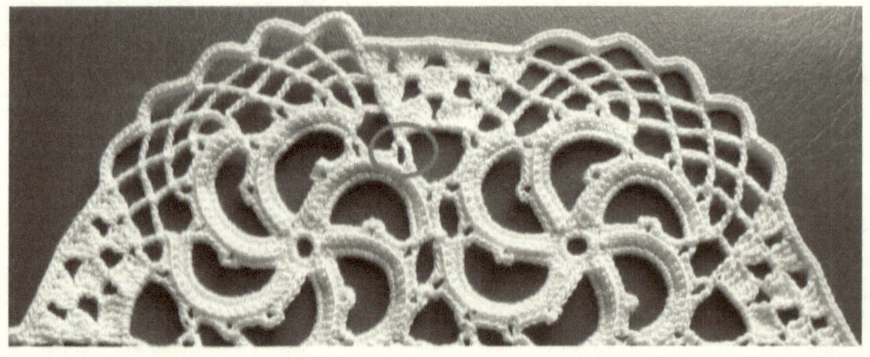

a. Working to the left, ch 7
b. [sl st into the tip of the arm to the left; (ch 7; sl st into the picot on the left) twice; ch 7] twice

c. sl st into the tip of the arm to the left; ch 7; sl st into the picot on the left; ch 7

d. sl st into the picot on the next medallion; ch 7

- Repeat Steps b through d around the doily 5 more times
- Repeat Steps b through c once more
- Sl st into where you joined the thread.

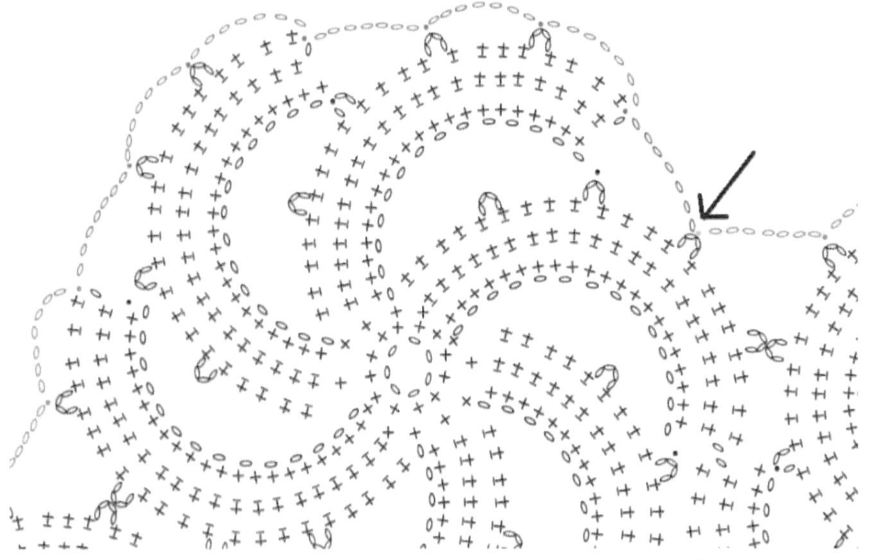

Round 2

e. sl st into the first 4 ch of the first round

f. [ch 7; sl st into the center chain of the next ch 7 loop from round 1] 7 times

g. tr 4 into the ch 7 joining the two medallions; ch 3; tr 4 into the same ch 7

h. sl st into the center ch of the next ch 7 of the first row

- Repeat Steps f through h around the edge of the doily, ending with a sl st into the base of

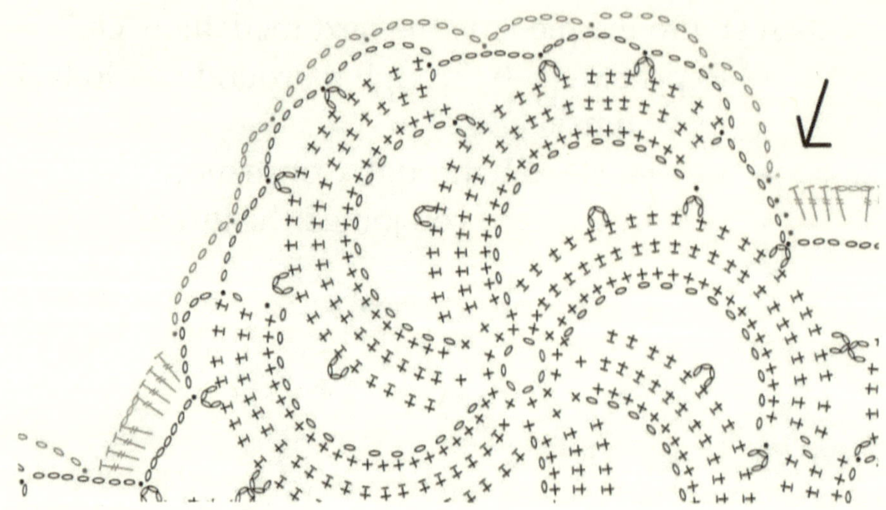

Round 3

i. sl st into the first 4 ch of the second round

j. [ch 7; sl st into the center chain of the next ch 7 loop from round 2] 6 times

k. tr 3 into the first tr made in the section; ch 2; tr 5 into the space between the tr in the second row; ch 2; tr 3 into the last tr made in the section in the previous row; sl st to the center chain of the next ch 7 loop

- Repeat Steps j through k around the edge of the doily, ending with a sl st into the base of the first ch 7 of Round 3

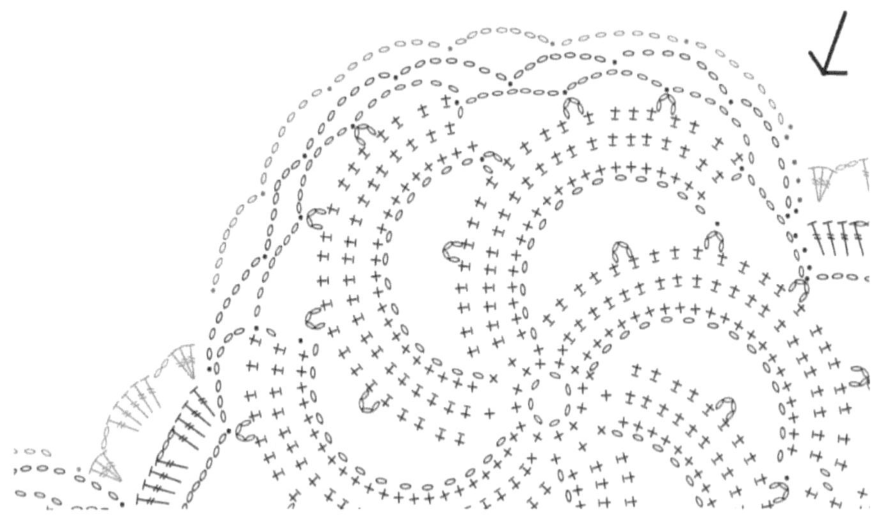

Round 4

l. sl st into the first 4 ch of the third round

m. [ch 7; sl st into the center chain of the next ch 7 loop from round 3] 5 times

n. tr 3 into the first tr made in the section; [ch 2; tr 4 into the next space] twice; ch 2; tr 3 into the last tr made in the section in the previous row; sl st to the center chain of the next ch 7 loop

- Repeat Steps m through n around the edge of the doily, ending with a sl st into the base of the first ch 7 of Round 4

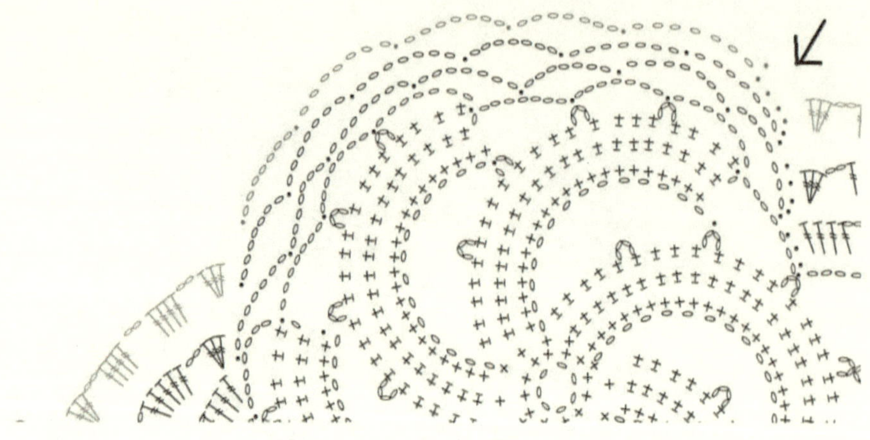

Round 5

    o. [sc 11 over the next ch 7] 5 times

    p. sc into the top of the next 3 tr; [sc 2 over the ch 2 space; sc into the top of the next four tr] twice; sc 2 over the ch 2 space; sc into the top of the next 3 tr

- Repeat Steps o through p around the edge of the doily, ending with a sl st into the base of the first sc of Round 5

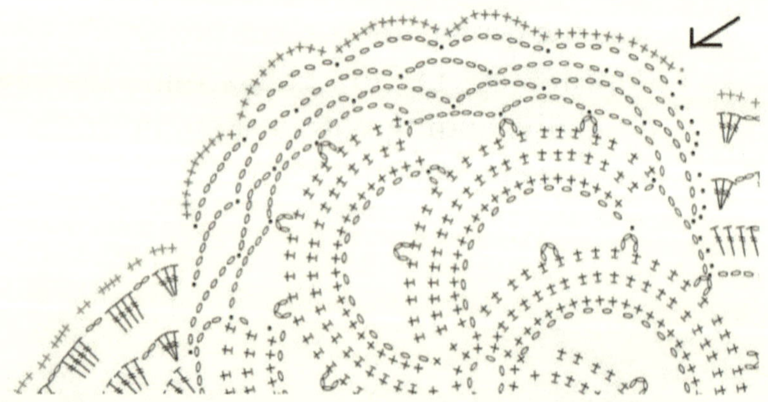

Pull thread through and cut leaving ~6" tail.
Weave in ends. ends.

Triangle Crochet Doily Pattern

As mentioned, crochet doilies are typically round but you can make them in other shapes as well, especially if you want to get a more contemporary look when using them for home decor. This is a three-sided (triangle-shaped) crochet doily pattern offered. We note that if you stop about two-thirds of the way through the pattern, you'll have a coaster-sized doily.

This is a thread crochet pattern but you could work it in a thicker yarn to make a triangle blanket or rug using this doily design.

How to make

1. Ch 5, join, ch 3 (counts as 1st dc) 11 dc in ring, join, 12dc.
2. Ch 3, dc in same sp as join, 2 dc in next dc and each dc around, 24dc.
3. Ch 3, dc in same st as join, *dc in next st, 2 dc in next st* around, join, 36dc.
4. Ch 6, sk 1 dc, dc in next st, *ch 3, sk 1 st, dc in next dc* around, join in 3rd ch of beg ch.
5. Ch 1, sc in same st as join, *3 sc in sp, sc in dc* around, join in 1st sc.
6. Ch 1, sc in join, *ch 8, sk 7 sc, sc in next st* around, join to 1st sc.
7. Ch 1, sc in same st as joining, 9dc in loop, sc in sc, 9dc in loop, sc in sc, 9sc in loop, sc in sc, *9dc in loop, sc in sc, 9 dc in loop, sc in sc, 9 sc in loop sc, in sc* around, join to 1st sc.
8. Ch 1, sc in same st as join, *9dc, ch 2, skip sc, 9dc. 11sc. * around, join.
9. Ch 1, sc in join, * 9 dc, ch 3, sc in sp, ch 3, 9dc, 11sc,*around, join in 1st sc.
10. Ch 1, sc in join, *9dc, ch 3, sc in sp (2 times) ch 3, 9dc, 11sc* around, join.
11. Ch 1, sc, *9dc, ch 3, sc in sp (3 times), ch 3, 9dc, 11sc* around, join.
12. Ch 1, sc, *9dc, ch 3, sc in sp (4 times), ch 3, 9dc, 11sc* join to 1st sc.
13. Ch 3, 9dc, *ch8, sc in 2nd sc, ch 8, dc in each dc and sc*, join.

14. Ch 3, *dc in each dc, 8 dc in sp, sc in sc, 8 dc in sp* around, join.

15. Ch 3, *dc in each dc to st before sc, tr in that st, in sc [dtr, ch4, st st to top of dtr, dtr, ch5, st st in top of dtr, dtr, ch 4, sl st in top of dtr, tr in next st* around, join.

16. Ch 1, sc, ch3, *sk 1 st, sc in next, ch3* around, to join ch 1 dc in 1st sc.

17. Ch 1, sc *ch3, sc in next sp around, to join ch 1 dc in last sp.

18. Ch 1, sc, ch3, sc in nex sp to three spaces at point, in each of these spaces [sc, ch 5, st st to list ch (picot), sc in same sp. Do that in next two spaces, ch 3, sc in next sp and each sp* to next point. Repeat 2 more times, join, fasten off.

Lace Triangle Doily Crochet Pattern

Rainbow Dandelion has a great array of crochet doily and motif patterns, many inspired by vintage designs but filled with modern flair. This one is a second example of how a doily can be done in the shape of a triangle.

The choice of yarn and the laciness of the open design give this a completely different style than the one above by Crochet Galore. One of the best things that you can do is to play around a lot with changing yarn types and hook sizes while working crochet doily patterns so that you can achieve a variety of different effects. You could make an entire wall art display of just doilies worked in this way.

How to make

Materials:

Worsted weight yarn pink (P).

Cardboard.

Clear plastic wrap.

Heavy spray starch.

Crochet hook: size needed to obtain gauge.

Gauge: 13dc = 6dc rows = 5cm (2'').

Abbreviations:

ch	chain	*rep*	repeat	*sl st(s)*	slip stitch(es)	*tr*	treble crochet
dc	double crochet	*sp*	space	*yo*	yarn over	*dc* *d*	double crochet decrease
lp(s)	loop(s)	*st(s)*	stitch (es)	*sc*	single crochet	*cl*	cluster

Size: 16 cm sides (you can resize it by using another yarn type)

Directions: (depend on the length and width you want you can change the number in pattern)

<u>Round 1:</u> right side, ch 7, sl st in 1st ch to form ring, ch 1, (2 sc, ch 15, 2 sc) 3 times in ring, sl st in 1st st.

Round 2: ch 1, sc in same sp, [ch 12; sc in 3rd ch of ch-15, ch 12, (sc in 6th ch, ch 15, sc in 10th ch, ch 12, sc in 13th ch, ch 12) of same ch-15; sc in next sc]*, [sc in next sc, rep *] twice, sl st in 1st st.

Round 3: ch 1, [sc in next 6 ch of ch-12, ch 2, sc in next 3 ch of same ch-12; sc in 4th ch of next ch-12, (sc in next 2 ch, ch 2, sc in next 4 ch) of same ch-12; sc in 3rd ch of next ch-15, (sc in next 5 ch, ch 2, sc in next 5 ch) of same ch-15; sc in 3rd ch of next ch-12, (sc in next 3 ch, ch 2, sc in next 3 ch) of same ch-12; sc in 4th ch of next ch-12, (sc in next 2 ch, ch 2, sc in next 6 ch) of same ch-12] around, sl st in 1st st.

Finish off.

Stiffened

- Cut a piece of cardboard larger than doily to be stiffened.
- Cover the cardboard with clear plastic wrap. Lay doily on the plastic, stretch out and pin into the correct shape.
- Generously spray with heavy spray starch. Allow to dry completely.
- This method allows for washing and re-starching whenever necessary.

Rings of Change Crochet Doily Pattern

Designer created one of the most popular crochet circle blanket designs ever, called the Rings of Change. They also show how you can use just the first third of that crochet pattern to create a beautiful, detailed doily. The doily can be made in a single solid color, as shown here, or worked in many, many colors like them larger designs usually are.

<u>**How to make**</u>
Hook size – J \ 6.00 mm

Yarn – Aran/Medium weight, Caron Simply Soft. If the 1st four rows of the pattern will not lay flat use a larger hook.

Yardage needed – 945yds./ 864m

Colors used in Rainbow version: Neon Coral, Neon Orange, Neon Yellow, Neon Green, Blue Mint, Grape & black. (r, o, y, g, b, p & blk)

Gauge – Rows 1-4 = 4.25″/ 10.7cm

Finished size - 40"/101cm

Abbreviations & Stitches used:

sk	skip
yo	yarn over
st(s)	stitch(es)
sp	space
sl st	slip stitch
ch	chain
sc	single crochet
hdc	half double crochet
dc	double crochet
edc	extended double crochet (made w/extra loop on bottom)

tr	treble crochet
dtr	double treble crochet
beg cl	beginning 2 double crochet cluster (stitch instructions above)
cl	cluster made from 2 dctog in same stitch (stitch instructions above)
v stitch	dc, ch 1, dc in same st
fpdc	front post double crochet
fphdc	front post half double crochet
fptr	front post treble crochet
sc inc	single crochet increase
hdc inc	half double crochet increase
dc inc	double crochet increase
tr inc	treble crochet increase
sc2tog	single crochet 2 together
sc3tog	single crochet 3 together
hdc2tog	half double crochet 2 together
dc2tog	double crochet 2 together
dc3tog	double crochet 3 together
dc5tog	double crochet 5 together
edc3tog	extended double crochet 3 together (made w/extra loop on top)
tr3tog	treble crochet 3 together
tr6tog	treble crochet 6 together
CS	Crocodile stitch
cl-v	Cluster V stitch (cl, ch 1, cl) in same st
XS	Cross stitch
BSS	Beginning Star stitch
SS	Star stitch **PS** Puff stitch
pc	Popcorn stitch

picot ch 4, sl st into 1st ch

<u>Row 1</u>: ch 4, counts as 1st tr. 23 tr in ring. Join with sl st in top ch of starting ch 4. 24 tr

<u>Row 2</u>: ch 1. sc in same stitch as join. 1 sc in each st around. Join with sl st in 1st sc. 24 sc

<u>Row 3</u>: ch 3, counts as 1st dc. dc in same st as join. *ch 2, sk next st, dc inc in next st* 11 times. ch 2. Join with sl st in top ch of starting ch 3. 24 dc & 12 ch 2

<u>Row 4</u>: ch 1. sc in same st as join, sc in next st. 2 sc in next ch 2 sp, *sc in next 2 sts, 2 sc in next ch 2 sp* 11 times Join with sl st in 1st sc. 48 sc

<u>Row 5</u>: ch 1. sc in same st as join. ch 2. *sk next sc, sc in next st, ch 2* 23 times. Join with sl st in 1st sc. 24 sc & 24 ch 2

<u>Row 6</u>: ch 1. sc in same st as join. (hdc & dc) in ch 2 sp. dc in next st, (tr, ch 2, tr) in ch 2 sp, dc in next st, (dc & hdc) in ch 2 sp, *sc in next st, (hdc & dc) in ch 2 sp. dc in next st, (tr, ch 2, tr) in ch 2 sp, dc in next st, (dc & hdc) in ch 2 sp* 7 times. Join with sl st in 1st sc.

<u>Row 7</u>: sl st in 1st hdc and 1st dc. ch 2, counts as 1st hdc. dc in next 2 sts, (2 tr, ch 2, 2 tr) in ch 2 sp, dc in next 2 sts, hdc in next st, of next 3 sts sc2tog using 1st and 3rd st skipping the 2nd st, *hdc in next st. dc in

next 2 sts, (2 tr, ch 2, 2 tr) in ch 2 sp, dc in next 2 sts, hdc in next st, of next 3 sts sc2tog using 1st and 3rd st skipping the 2nd st* 7 times. Join with sl st in top ch of starting ch 2.

Row 8: ch 1, sc in same stitch as join. Sc in next 4 sts. (2 sc, ch 2, 2 sc) in ch 2 sp, sc in next 5 sts, sk next st. *sc in next 5 sts, (2 sc, ch 2, 2 sc) in ch 2 sp, sc in next 5 sts, sk next st* 7 times. Join with sl st in 1st sc. 112 sc & 8 ch 2

Row 9: ch 4, counts as 1st tr. tr in next st, *dc2tog, hdc in next 2 sts, sc in next st, (sc, ch 2, sc) in ch 2 sp, sc in next st, hdc in next 2 sts, dc2tog, tr in next 4 sts* 7 times. dc2tog, hdc in next 2 sts, sc in next st, (sc, ch 2, sc) in ch 2 sp, sc in next st, hdc in next 2 sts, dc2tog, tr in next 2 sts. Join with sl st in top ch of starting ch 4.

Row 10: ch 3, counts as 1st dc. dc in next 6 sts. *(dc, ch 2, dc) in ch 2 sp, dc in next 7 sts. 4 ch picot, dc in next 7 sts* 7 times. (dc, ch 2, dc) in ch 2 sp, dc in next 7 sts. 4 ch picot. Join with sl st in top ch of starting ch 3. 128 dc, 8 ch 2 & 8 picot

Row 11 NOTE: Do not count sl st when skipping sts for this row.
Row 11: Counting ch 3 as 1st dc, sl st over to the 4th dc. ch 1, sc in same st, ch 1, sk next st, sc in next st. *sk next 2 sts, (4 dc, ch 1, 4 dc) in ch 2 sp, sk next 2 sts, sc in next st, ch 1, sk next st, sc in next st, sk next 3 sts,

[tr, ch 1] 6 times in picot, tr in picot, sk next 3 sts, sc in next st, ch 1, sk next st, sc in next st, * 7 times. sc in next st, sk next 2 sts, (4 dc, ch 1, 4 dc) in ch 2 sp, sk next 2 sts, sc in next st, ch 1, sk next st, sc in next st, [tr, ch 1] 6 times in picot, tr in picot, sk next 3 sts. Join with sl st in 1st sc.

Row 12 NOTE: When skipping the groups of sts make sure you sk all 5 of the sts in the group. "sk: next tr, sc, ch 1, sc & dc" and "sk: next dc, sc, ch 1, sc & tr"

Row 12: sl st over to 2nd dc of corner. ch 1, sc in same st. *hdc in next st, dc in next st, (dc, ch 1, dc, ch 1, dc) in ch 1 sp, dc in next st, hdc in next st, sc in next st. sk: next dc, sc, ch 1, sc & tr, (cl in ch 1 sp, ch 2, sk next st) 5 times, cl in ch 1 sp, sk: next tr, sc, ch 1, sc & dc, sc in next st* 7 times. hdc in next st, dc in next st, (dc, ch 1, dc, ch 1, dc) in ch 1 sp, dc in next st, hdc in next st, sc in next st. sk: next dc, sc, ch 1, sc & tr, (cl in ch 1 sp, ch 2, sk next st) 5 times, cl in ch 1 sp. sk: next tr, sc, ch 1, sc & dc. Join with sl st in 1st sc.

Row 13: sl st over to next st, ch 1, sc in same st. sc in next 2 sts, sc in ch1 sp, sc in next st, sc in next ch1 sp, sc in next 3 sts, sk next: st & cl, (2 sc in ch 2, sk cl) 5 times, sk next cl & st, *sc in next 3 sts, sc in next ch1 sp, sc in next st, sc in next ch1 sp, sc in next 3 sts, sk next: st & cl, (2 sc in ch 2, sk cl) 5 times, sk next st* 7 times. Join with sl st in 1st sc. 152 sc

Row 14: ch 3, counts as 1st dc. dc in next st, *hdc in next st, sc in next 3 sts, hdc in next st, dc in next 4 sts, hdc in next st, sc in next 4 sts, hdc in next st, dc in next 4 sts* 7 times. hdc in next st, sc in next 3 sts, hdc in next st, dc in next 4 sts, hdc in next st, sc in next 4 sts, hdc in next st, dc in next 2 sts. Join with sl st in top ch of starting ch 3.

Row 15: ch 1, sc in same st. sc in next 6 sts, *sc inc in next st, sc in next 7 sts* repeat 18 times. sc in last st. Join with sl st in 1st sc. 170 sc

Row 16: ch 2, counts as 1st hdc. hdc in next 8 sts, hdc inc in next st. *hdc in next 9 sts, hdc inc in next st* 15 times. hdc in next 10 sts. Join with sl st in top ch of starting ch 2. 186 hdc

Row 17: TURN. On Wrong Side, ch 1, sc in same st as join. sc in each stitch around. Join with sl st in 1st sc. 186 sc

Row 18 NOTE: Allow all tr to protrude to Right Side.

Row 18: On Wrong Side, ch 1, sc in same st as join. *tr in next st, sc in next st* 92 times. tr in last st. Join with sl st in 1st sc. 93 tr & 93 sc

Row 19: On Wrong Side, ch 1, sc in same st as join. sc in each stitch around. Join with sl st in 1st sc. 186 sc

Row 20: TURN. On Right Side, ch 2, counts as 1st hdc. hdc in each stitch around. Join with sl st in top ch of starting ch 2. 186 hdc

Row 21: ch 1, sc in same st as join. *ch 2, sk next st, sc in next st* 92 times. ch 2. Join with sl st in 1st sc. 93 sc & 93 ch 2

Row 22: sl st into chain 2 sp, ch 1, sc in chain 2 sp. *ch 3, sk next st, sc in ch 2* 92 times. ch 3. Join with sl st in 1st sc. 93 sc & 93 ch 3

Row 23: sl st into chain 3 sp, ch 1, sc in chain 3 sp. *ch 4, sk next st, sc in ch 3* 92 times. ch 4. Join with sl st in 1st sc. 93 sc & 93 ch 4

Row 24: sl st into chain 4 sp, ch 1, sc in chain 4 sp. *ch 5, sk next st, sc in ch 4* 92 times. ch 5. Join with sl st in 1st sc.93 sc & 93 ch 5

Row 25: sl st into ch 5 sp, ch 1, sc in ch 5 sp. *ch 3, sk next st, sc in ch 5 sp* 92 times. ch 3. Join with sl st in 1st sc. 93 sc & 93 ch 3

Row 26: sl st into ch 3 sp, ch 1. 3 sc in same ch 3 sp, *sk next st, 3 sc in ch 3 sp* 91 times. sc in next st, 3 sc in next ch 3 sp. Join with sl st in 1st sc. 280 sc

Row 27: ch 1, sc in same st as join. sc in each stitch

around. Join with sl st in 1st sc. 280 sc

Row 28 TIP: When making 2nd dc of cross stitch, yo then bend 1st dc made forward and go into the skipped st from the front as normal. The 1st dc stays in the front, the 2nd dc is made behind the 1st dc.

Row 28: ch 3. dc in st before starting ch 3. *sk next st, dc in next st, dc in skipped st* Cross stitch made. Cross stitch around. Join with sl st in top ch of starting ch 3. 140 cross stitch

Row 29: ch 3, counts as 1st dc. dc in next 12 sts, dc inc in next st, *dc in next 13 sts, dc inc in next st* 19 times. Join with sl st in top ch of starting ch 3.
300 dc

Row 30: ch 2, sk next st, dc in next st, ch 3. *sk next st, of next 3 sts dc2tog using 1st and 3rd sts, ch 3* 74 times. Join with sl st in top of the 1st inverted V stitch. 75 inv V st & 75 ch 3

<u>Row 31 TIP</u>: After making this row, to straighten out the legs of the inverted V sts, pinch any ch 3 of row 30 between sts with both hands and gently pull outwards. Do this on each ch 3 around to snug the sts up next to the inverted V stitch of row 30.

<u>Row 31</u>: sl st backwards to previous ch 3 ch 2, sk next st, dc in next ch 3 sp, ch 3.dc2tog around next dc2tog placing 1st half of dc2tog on the ch 3 sp to the right of the dc2tog of the previous row and the 2nd half of the dc2tog on the ch 3sp to the left of the dc2tog of the previous row, ch 3* 75 times. Join with sl st in top of 1st inverted V stitch. 75 inv V st & 75 ch 3

<u>Row 32</u>: sl st over to ch 3 sp, ch 1, *4 sc in ch 3 sp, sk next st* 75 times. Join with sl st in 1st sc. 300 sc

<u>Row 33</u>: ch 1, sc in same st. sc in next 8 sts, sc inc in next st, *sc in next 9 sts, sc inc in next st* 29 times. Join with sl st in 1st sc. 330 sc

<u>Row 34</u>: ch 1, sc in same st. ch 4, sk next 2 sts, sc in next st, sk next 3 sts, 5 tr in next st, sk next 3 sts, *sc in next st, ch 4, sk next 2 sts, sc in next st, sk next 3 sts, 5 tr in next st, sk next 3 sts* 29 times. Join with sl st in 1st sc. 30 tr fans, 60 sc & 30 ch 4

<u>Row 35</u>: sl st into ch 4 sp. ch 1, *sc in ch 4 sp, sk next st, dc inc in next 2 sts, ch 3, sc in next st, ch 3, dc inc in next 2 sts, sk next st* 30 times. Join with sl st in 1st

sc. 240 dc, 60 sc & 60 ch 3

<u>Row 36:</u> ch 4, counts as 1st tr, 4 tr in same st, sk next 4 sts, sc in ch 3 sp, ch 4, *sk next st, sc in ch 3 sp, sk next 4 sts, 5 tr in next st, sk next 4 sts, sc in ch 3 sp, ch 4* 29 times. sk next st, sc in ch 3 sp. Join with sl st in top ch of starting ch 4. 30 tr fans, 60 sc & 30 ch 4

<u>Row 37:</u> ch 3, counts as 1st dc, dc in same st as join, dc inc in next st, ch 3, sc in next st, ch 3, dc inc in next 2 sts, sk next st, sc in ch 4 sp, sk next st. *dc inc in next 2 sts, ch 3, sc in next st, ch 3, dc inc in next 2 sts, sk next st, sc in ch 4 sp, sk next st* 29 times. Join with sl st in top ch of starting ch 3. 240 dc, 60 sc & 60 ch 3

<u>Row 38:</u> sl st over to 1st dc before ch 3 sp. ch 3, counts as 1st dc, *(3 dc, 2 tr) in next ch 3 sp, ch 1, (2 tr, 3 dc) in next ch 3 sp, dc in next st, dc2tog, dc3tog, dc2tog, dc in next st* 30 times. (3 dc, 2 tr) in next ch 3 sp, ch 1, (2 tr, 3 dc) in next ch 3 sp, dc in next st, dc2tog, dc3tog, dc2tog. Join with sl st in top ch of starting ch 3.

<u>Row 39:</u> ch 2, counts as 1st hdc. hdc in next 5 sts, *(hdc, ch 3, hdc) in ch 1 sp, hdc in next 6 sts, sc3tog, hdc in next 6 sts* 29 times. (hdc, ch 3, hdc) in ch 1 sp, hdc in next 6 sts, sc3tog. Join with sl st in top of starting ch 2. 420 hdc, 30 ch 3 & 30 sc3tog
<u>ROW 40 NOTE:</u> The 1st hdc after the 9 tr might be buried but counts as 1 of the 4 skipped hdc before the

sl st in the 5th st. It can be easier counting sk sts backwards from place that next set of sts will be.

Row 40: Counting starting ch 2 as 1st hdc, sl st over to 3rd hdc. *sk next 4 sts, (tr, ch 1) 8 times in ch 3 sp, tr in same ch 3 sp. sk next 4 sts, sl st in next st, sk next 2 sts, 5 dc in next st, sk next 2 sts, sl st in next st* 30 times using last sl st to join at 1st sl st before 1st tr. 270 tr, 240 ch 1, 150 dc & 60 sl st

ROW 41 NOTE: Do not count sl sts when counting sk sts for this row.

Row 41: sl st into 1st tr, ch 3, counts as 1st dc, (2 dc in next ch 1 sp, dc in next st) repeat 8 times, sk next 2 sts, sl st in next st, *sk next 2 sts, dc in 1st tr, (2 dc in next ch 1 sp, dc in next st) 8 times, sk next 2 sts, sl st in next st* 29 times. sk next 2 sts. Join with sl st in top of starting ch 3. Fasten off. 750 dc

Row 42: Counting starting ch 3 as 1st dc join yarn in 13th dc of any arch, ch 1, sc in same st. sc in next 9 sts, sl st in next st, sk next 5 sts, sl st in next st, *sc in next 19 sts, sl st in next st, sk next 5 sts, sl st in next st* 29 times. sc in next 9 sts. Join with sl st in 1st sc. Fasten off. 570 sc & 60 sl st

Seasonal Crochet Doily Pattern

This doily crochet pattern is one of the best contemporary doily designers. It was designed as a Thanksgiving crochet pattern, but it would certainly work throughout the fall season, and you could even adapt the coloring to make it a doily you could use in your home all year long.

This designer has a large array of doily crochet patterns for all different types of holidays so take some time to peruse through their blog and find the doily design that is right for you!

<u>**How to make**</u>

Size: About 15" across

Skill Level: Intermediate   For those who are familiar with working with size 10 thread and steel hooks, and who have a thorough understanding of the basics of crochet

Special Stitches

For **2 tr cluster:** (yo 2 times, insert hook in st or sp indicated, yo, pull lp through, yo, work off 2 lps, yo, work off next 2 lps) 2 times, yo, pull through all 3 lps on hook

For **3 tr cluster:** (yo 2 times, insert hook in st or sp indicated, yo, pull lp through, yo, work off 2 lps, yo, work off next 2 lps) 3 times, yo, pull through all 4 lps on hook

For **cluster shell (cl shell):** work (3 dc cl, ch 2, 3 dc cl) in st or ch sp indicated

Materials For Doily A:
- Size 10 Crochet Cotton Thread:
    100 yds. each Cream and Yellow
    75 yds each Green, Rust and Orange
- Heavy Spray Starch
- Size 7 *(1.65mm)* Steel Crochet Hook

Materials For Doily B:
- Size 10 Crochet Cotton Thread:
    100 yds. each Cream and Orange
    75 yds each Green, Rust and Yellow
- Heavy Spray Starch
- Size 7 *(1.65mm)* Steel Crochet Hook

Doily A

Rnd 1: With green, ch 2, 9 sc in 2nd ch from hook, join with sl st in first sc. Fasten off. *(9 sc made)*

Rnd 2: Join yellow with sl st in first sc, (ch 3, **2 tr cl-** *see Special Stitches)* in same st as joining *(counts as first 3-tr cl)*, ch 5, **(3 tr cluster-** *see Special Stitches-* in next sc, ch 5) around, join with sl st in top of 2-tr cl. Fasten off. *(9 3-tr cls, 9 ch-5 sps made)*

Rnd 3: Join green with sc in first ch-5 sp, (2 sc, ch 3, 3 sc) in same sp as joining, (3 sc, ch 3, 3 sc) in each ch-5 sp around, join with sl st in first sc. Fasten off.

Rnd 4: Join orange with sl st in first ch-3 sp, (ch 3, 2 tr cl, ch 3, 3 tr cl, ch 3, 3 tr cl, ch 3) in same sp as joining, (3 tr cl, ch 3) 3 times in each ch-3 sp around, join with sl st in top of ch-2 cl. Fasten off.

Rnd 5: Join green with sc in first ch-3 sp, 2 sc in same sp as joining, ch 1, (3 sc in next ch-3 sp, ch 1) around, join with sl st in first sc. Fasten off.

Rnd 6: Join cream with sc in first ch-1 sp, ch 5, (sc in next ch-1 sp, ch 5) around, join with sl st in first sc.

Rnd 7: Sl st to center of first ch-5 sp (ch 1, sc) in first ch-5 sp, ch 5, (sc in next ch-5 sp, ch 5) around, join with sl st in first sc.

Rnd 8: Sl st to center of first ch-5 sp, (ch 1, sc) in first ch-5 sp, ch 6, (sc in next ch-5 sp, ch 6) around, join with sl st in first sc.

Rnd 9: Sl st to center of first ch-6 sp, (ch 1, sc) in first ch-6 sp, ch 6, (sc in next ch-6 sp, ch 6) around, join with sl st in first sc.

Rnd 10: Sl st to center of first ch-6 sp, (ch 1, sc) in first ch-6 sp, ch 7, (sc in next ch-6 sp, ch 7) around, join with sl st in first sc.

Rnd 11: Sl st to center of first ch-7 sp, (ch 1, sc) in first ch-7 sp, ch 7, (sc in next ch-7 sp, ch 7) around, join with sl st in first sc. Fasten off.

Rnd 12: Join green with sc in first ch-7 sp, (3 sc, ch 3, 4 sc) in same sp as joining, (4 sc, ch 3, 4 sc) in each ch sp around, join. Fasten off.

Rnd 13: Join rust with sl st in first ch-3 sp, (ch 3, 2 tr cl, ch 3, 3 tr cl, ch 3, 3 tr cl, ch 3) in same sp as joining, (3 tr cl, ch 3) 3 times in each ch-3 sp around, join with sl st in top of 2-tr cl. Fasten off.

Rnd 14: Join green with sc in first ch-3 sp, 2 sc in same sp as joining, ch 1, (3 sc, ch 1) in each ch-3 sp around, join with sl st in first sc. Fasten off.

Rnd 15: Join cream with sc in first ch-1 sp, ch 5, (sc in next ch-1 sp, ch 5) around, join with sl st in first sc.

Rnds 16&17: Sl st to center of first ch-5 sp (ch 1, sc) in first ch-5 sp, ch 5, (sc in next ch-5 sp, ch 5) around, join with sl st in first sc.

Rnd 18: Sl st to center of first ch-5 sp, (ch 1, sc) in first ch-5 sp, ch 6, (sc in next ch-5 sp, ch 6) around, join with sl st in first sc.

Rnds 19& 20: Sl st to center of first ch-6 sp, (ch 1, sc) in first ch-6 sp, ch 6, (sc in next ch-6 sp, ch 6) around, join with sl st in first sc.

Rnd 21: Sl st to center of first ch-6 sp, (ch 1, sc) in first ch-6 sp, ch 7, (sc in next ch-6 sp, ch 7) around, join with sl st in first sc. Fasten off.

Rnd 22: Join green with sc in first ch-7 sp, ch 3, (3 tr cl, ch 3) 6 times in next ch-7 sp, sc in next ch-7 sp, ch 5, *sc in next ch-7 sp, ch 3, (3 tr cl, ch 3) 6 times in next ch-7 sp, sc in next ch-7 sp, ch 5; repeat from * around, join with sl st in first sc. Fasten off.

Rnd 23: To complete this round, work Steps A-F:

A: Join yellow with sc in first ch-5 sp, ch 3, skip next ch-3 sp, (**cl shell**-*see Special Stitches*-in next ch-3 sp, ch 3, sc in next ch-3 sp, ch 3) 2 times;

B: cl shell in next ch-3 sp, ch 3, skip next ch-3 sp;

C: sc in next ch-5 sp, ch 3, skip next ch-3 sp;

D: (cl shell in next ch-3 sp, ch 3, sc in next ch-3 sp, ch 3) 2 times;

E: cl shell in next ch-3 sp, ch 3, skip next ch-3 sp;

F: repeat Steps C, D, and E around, join with sl st in first sc. Fasten off.

Rnd 24: Join rust with sc in first ch-3 sp, ch 3, (sc, ch 3, sc) in ch-2 sp of next cl shell, ch 3, sc in next ch-3 sp, *sc in next ch-3 sp, ch 3, (sc, ch 3, sc) in ch-2 sp of next cl shell, ch 3, sc in next ch-3 sp; repeat from * around, join. Fasten off.

T-Shirt Yarn Doily Rug Crochet Pattern

Crochet In Paternoster is always making wonderful things using t-shirt yarn. This doily rug is a terrific example of that. Their crochet pattern could be a traditional doily if it were worked in thread with a small hook but instead it is worked with thick, chunky, beautifully pink t-shirt yarn and a large hook that creates a cushy circular rug.

Switch out any doily pattern for this type of yarn and see what items you can create!

How to make

Stitches used: (US terminology)
ch = chain
sc = single crochet
hdc = half double crochet
dc = double crochet
ss = slip stitch
V-stitch = (1 dc, ch 2, 1 dc). In some of the rounds, the V-stitches have 3 chains in-between the dc's. The first V-stitch in a round has 3 chains which counts as a dc. Rounds are closed with a slip stitch in the 3rd chain of that beginning 3 ch. NB, some rounds are closed with a slip stitch into the first V.

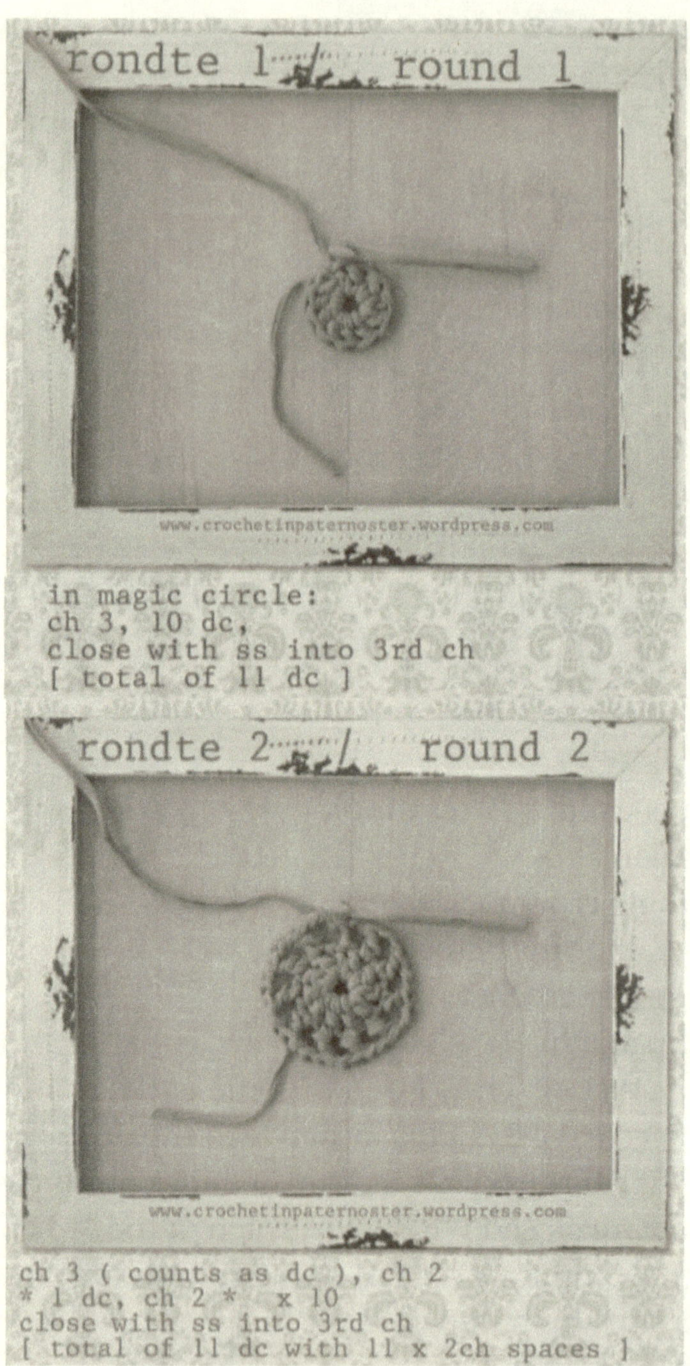

in magic circle:
ch 3, 10 dc,
close with ss into 3rd ch
[total of 11 dc]

ch 3 (counts as dc), ch 2
* 1 dc, ch 2 * x 10
close with ss into 3rd ch
[total of 11 dc with 11 x 2ch spaces]

round 3

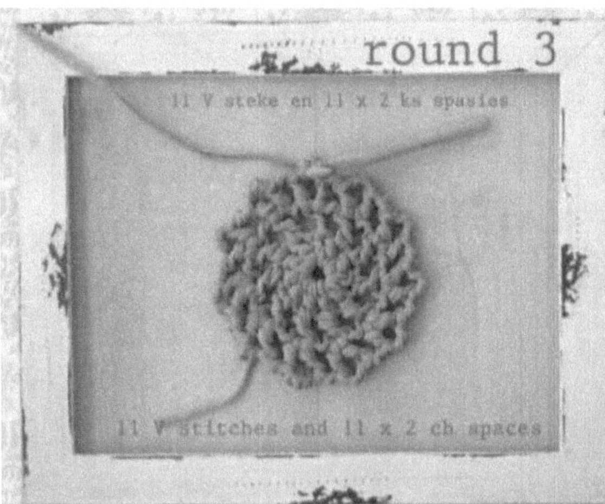

V stitches
into your
dc's

with 2 ch
in between

close with ss into 3rd beginning chain

rondte 4   round 4

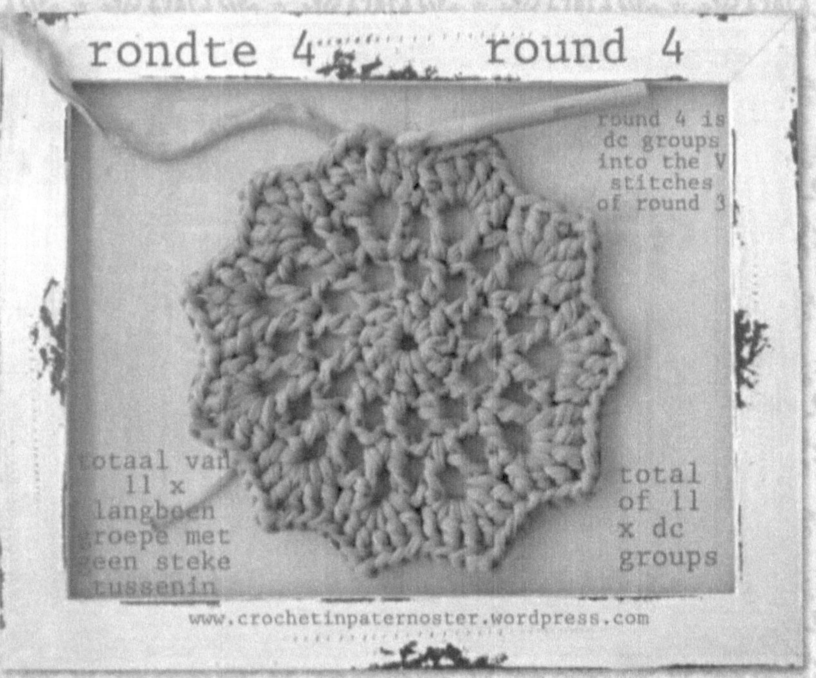

start with ch 3, 2 dc, ch 2, 3 dc.

* 3 dc, ch2, 3 dc * all around and
close with ss into 3rd ch

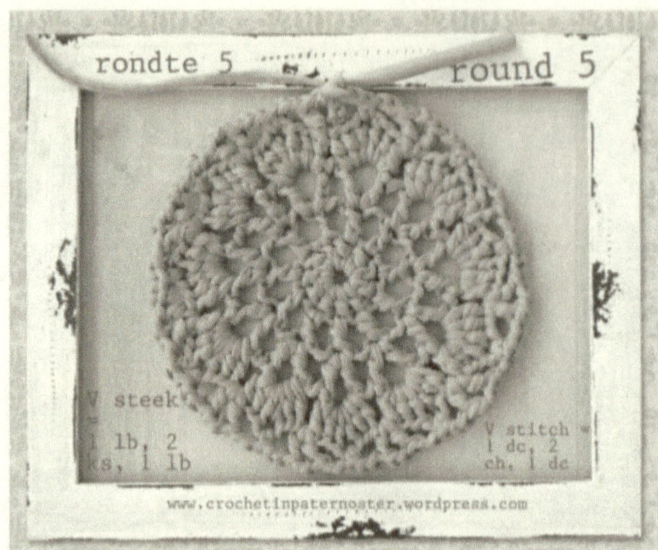

V stitch in the space in
between the dc clusters, ch 2,
sc in the 2 ch space. close
with ss in V stitch.

this round is sc's into the V
stitches with 8ch loops in between

1 sc, ch 8 all around

close with ss in beginning sc

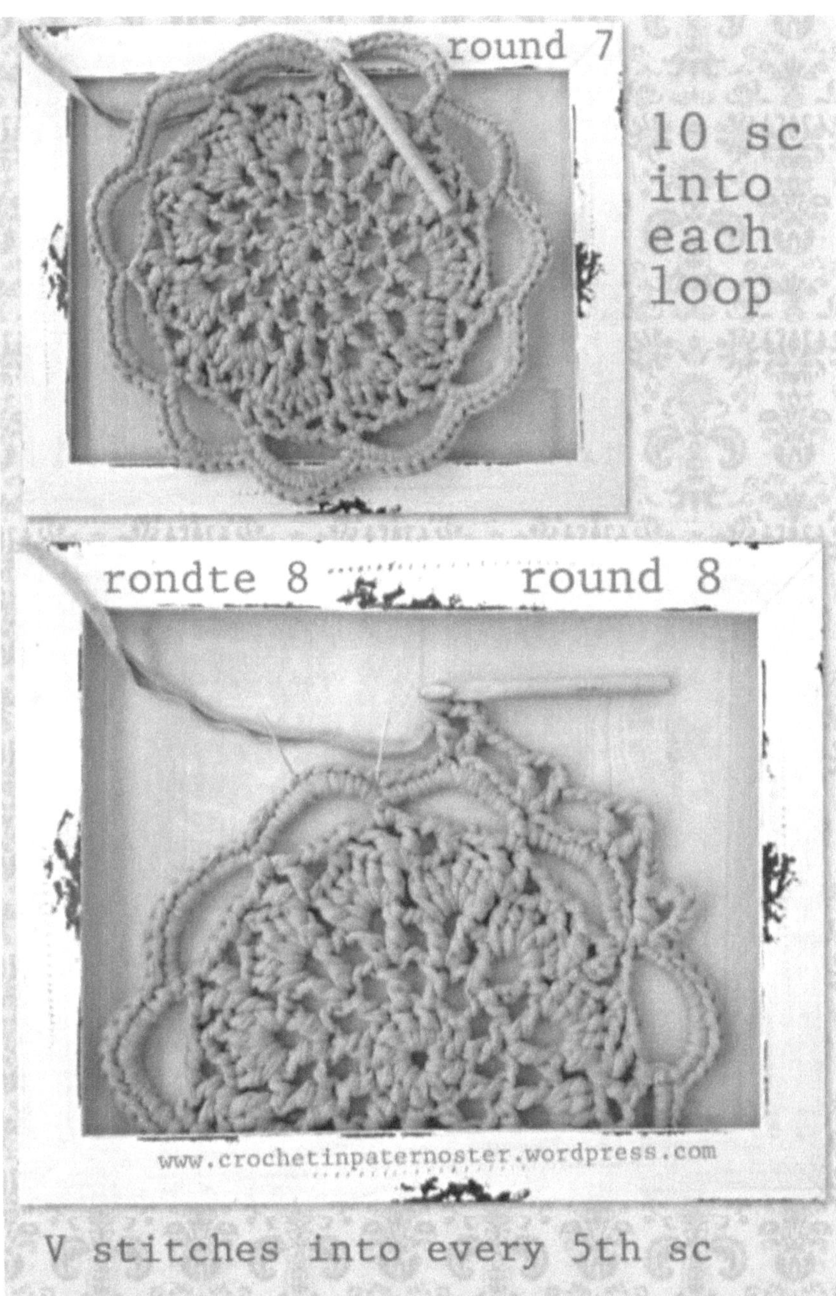

V stitches into every 5th sc

V = (1dc, ch 3, 1dc) with ch 3 in between

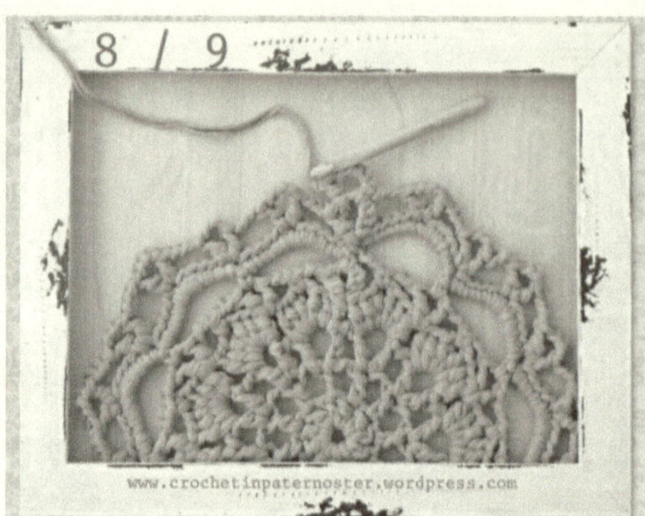

to close round 8:
ss into your beginning V stitch
to start round 9:
ch 6 (counts as 1 dc and 3 ch), 1 dc
this is your first V-stitch for the
round.

rondte 9 round 9

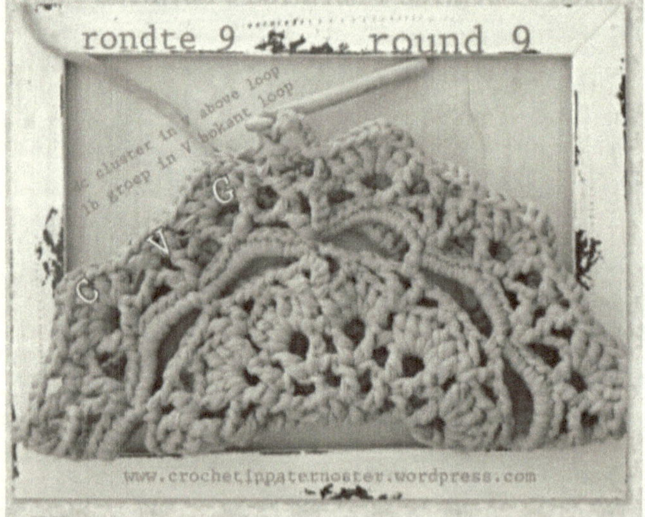

V V-stitch (1dc, ch 3, 1 dc)

C and then into the V above the loop:
3 dc, ch 3, 3 dc (cluster)

same as round 9, but with 1 ch
between your V's and clusters

V-stitch (1 dc, ch 3, 1 dc) ch 1,
3 dc, ch 3, 3 dc, ch 1 all around

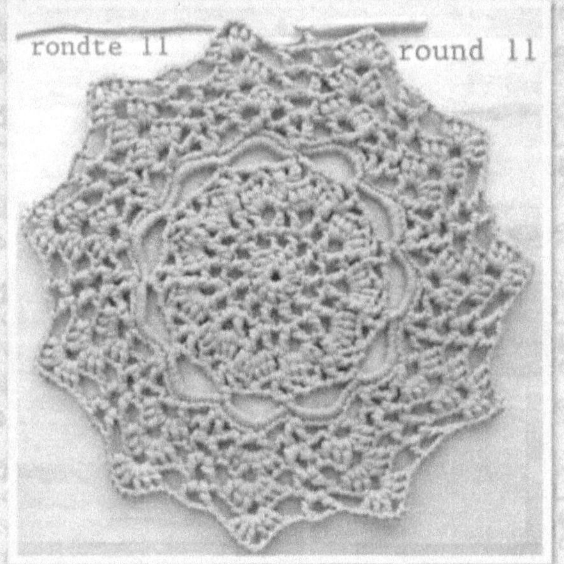

same as round 10, but with ch 2 between your
V-stitches and your dc clusters

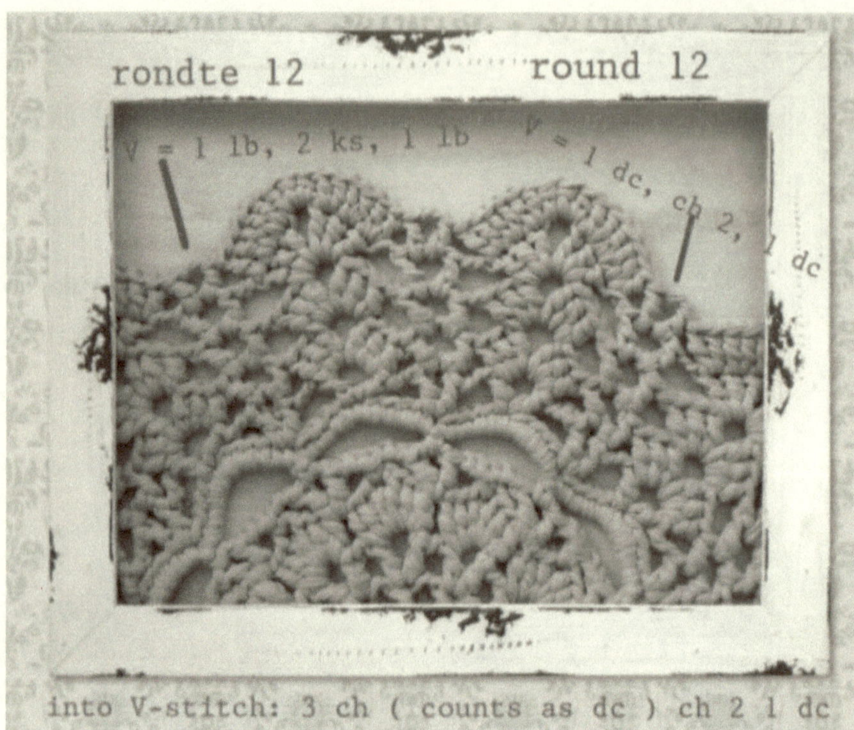

into V-stitch: 3 ch (counts as dc) ch 2 1 dc

into dc stitches: 2 dc
into 3 ch space: 3 hdc
into dc stitches: 2 dc

V into previous round V